Digital and Computer Forensics
Examiner: Cyber Security Forensic
Analyst, Job Interview Bottom Line
Questions and Answers: Your Basic
Guide to Acing Any Forensic
Technology Services Job Interview

Keywords

Digital forensics, computer forensics, network forensics, cyber forensics, digital evidence, Computer evidence, computer crime, incident response, Linux forensics, Windows Forensics, computer forensic tools, computer forensics procedures, disk forensics, media Forensics, intrusion forensics, intrusion detection systems.

It's for the following Job interviews:

Forensic Examiner
Computer Forensics Analyst
Digital Forensics Analyst/Investigator
Computer Forensics Analyst
Senior Computer Forensics Engineer
Information Forensics Investigator
Digital Forensic Examiner
Forensics Analyst / Engineer
Digital Forensics Investigator

Sector: Information Technology

Why this Book:

It will help you to convey powerful and useful technical
information about Digital Forensics to the employer
successfully.
This book tries to bring together all the important Digital
Forensics Investigator interview information for a Last-minute
interview preparation in as low as 60 minutes.
It covers technical, non-technical, HR and Personnel questions
and also UNIX commands used for forensics.
You will learn to practice mock interviews and answers for a
Digital Forensics Investigator job interview questions related to
the following:

Perform computer forensic examinations, Analysis &
Investigation
Collection and preservation of electronic evidence
Virus prevention and remediation

Recover active, system and hidden filenames with date/time stamp information

Detect and recover erased files, file slack.

Crack password protected files

Metadata extraction and analysis by open source (Linux & Windows)

Forensic tools and Products such as encase

Discover, analyze, diagnose, report on malware events

Files and network intrusion and vulnerability issues, firewalls and proxies

Access control, encryption and security event log analysis

Advanced knowledge of the Windows operating system (including registry, file system, memory and kernel level operations)

Receiving, reviewing and maintaining the integrity and proper custody of all evidence

Inventory and preservation of the seized digital evidence

Network security, cyber security, data protection and privacy forensic investigation

Evidence Collection and Management

Guidelines for Evidence Collection and Archiving

Etc...Etc...

Index:

Explain How a computer Boots?

What is a file that contains vital information for several aspects of a computer?

Explain why Firewalls can be used to detect Forensic Evidence for malicious attacks?

In case of an attack on computer or network what logs you should collect?

Explain Distributed Denial of Service Attacks?

How to prevent a Distributed Denial of Service (DDoS) attack?

How to prevent foot printing?

What is stealth rule?

What is Full disk encryption?

How to detecte illegal software distribution?

How many ports are in TCP/IP Protocol Suite

What is brute force attacks and how to prevent it?

What kind of IP is assigned to ISP dial up accounts and how to track it?

What is Triage?

Explain Secure Hash Algorithm?

How to store the entire partition?

How to perform Forensic log parsing of IIS or a web hack?

How to see what ip addresses attempted to log into your FTP site?

Explain your experience using the inode structure?

Explain The Sleuth Kit?

How to ensure time synchronization on Logs?

How determine the integrity of a file or a disk on Linux?

Can you explain the difference between primary & secondary transfers?

As a Digital Forensics Investigator what you think affects transfer?

What is ISFA Code of Ethics?

Explain Diffie-Hellman Encryption Algorithms?

What authority IRT - Leader has?

Explain the use of a honey pot in Forensic?

Explain the Foreign Intelligence Surveillance Act of 1978? How it relates to forensic?

The Counterfeit Access Device and Computer Fraud and Abuse Act of 1986 Prohibits what?

What is Computer Fraud and Abuse Act? How it affects Forensic?

What is USA PATRIOT Act? Whats for Forensic investigation?

Explain File Slack? What Forensic information you can gather from it?

Explain RAM Slack? What Forensic information you can gather from it?

What is MS Windows swap file? What Forensic information you can gather from it?

How to prevent unauthorized access to the sensitive data stored on your computer?

Explain Triple Data Encryption Algorithm?

What do forensic audit use?

As a first responder how, why and when to collect evidence in the clipboard ?

What is volatile evidence and how to collect volatile live evidence?

Can you check evidence that keeps changing? What are the Guidelines for Evidence

Collection and Archiving? Explain the order of Volatility.

What is the first rule in digital forensics?

What have you done in forensic first stages of an investigation?

What are the two tests for digital evidence to survive in a court of law?

Do you have any experience in bypassing Windows security?

What are the requirements for a forensic Bootable Compact Disc?

Name a forensic operating system?

What can you do to disable passwords on the BIOS?

Is it possible to recover files deleted from trashcan? How?

How to find users web activity on internet explorer?

Which tools have you used for the collection of evidence?

Which Key loggers have you worked with?

What to compare between clone and the source drive?

Is it possible to detect and prevent Key loggers?

Yes.

What is Rootkit?

How to Detect Rootkits?

Explain Hardware Keylogger?

Hardware Keylogger types?

Name a few Keyloggers?

What is required for submitting forensic evidence in a testimony?

What are the classes of computer forensics tools?

What are the three forms Challenges to the authenticity of computer records can take?

What you can see in the IDS logs?

Name a few intrusion detection systems?

What is foot printing? What is port scanning?

What is Penetration Testing?

Explain Rules of evidence?

How you can show that the evidence was not tampered?

What is Deposition?

Explain what you know about SMTP?

Why to use Reverse DNS?

Name most common email protocols?

How to identify a TCP connection? List some common ports?

Explain why Host-based IDS miss DOS attacks? Whats the Solution?

Explain your experience with Chain of Custody?

How will you maintain an accurate and complete chain of custody?

Do you have any experience in Identifying and Mitigating source address spoofing?

Explain Spoofing?

How to determine whether your systems might be vulnerable to denial of service (DoS) attacks? How to prevent it?

Explain your experience with Spoofing Prevention Methods?

Which tools have you used to recover files?

How to Delete or neutralize computer viruses?

What is ARP Poisoning (Man-in-the-Middle) Attack?

What port is for LDAP?

Explain the TCP three-way handshake?

What is black hat hacker?

How to Detect and recover erased files?

How to crack password protected files?

Explain your experience with Metadata?

How to perform Metadata extraction and analysis?

Explain the architecture of Metadata extraction Tools?

How to acquire a forensically protected disk image?

Have you worked with Hachoir?

EnCase uses which two methods for identifying file types?

How proficient are you in open source forensic tools?

Explain Host Protected Area? How to check it?

What is DCO?

Which Anti Forensic tool can modify Timestamps?

What is the length of a Dword?

What is found in EnCase Case File?

What are the various .ini Files in EnCase?

How to take a memory dump with Knoppix-STD tools?

How to check a UNIX system for a buffer overflow attack?

What are the components of Encase Evidence file?

Explain Zero day attacks?

List the rules of evidence?

How to examine which hosts has been connected to by Telnet?

How to see Forensic Evidence for malicious attacks on a Firewall?

List Forensic Artifacts in a Browser?

Explain PPM – Probabilistic Packet Marking?

Explain steganography?

Which ports used by Windows are Most Vulnerable?

Which ports NetBIOS uses over TCP?

Which are popular Email Ports?

Name 2 most used cryptographic hash functions?

What is FTP, In terms of security what makes it difficult to control the File Transfer Protocol (FTP) via a firewall rule set or packet filter?

Explain various components of Disks?

Explain the I/O Data Path?

Explain your experience with DNS, and what you did to make it secure?

How does DNSSec provide greater security?

What are the tasks associated with DNSSEC?

What is SMTP, Which port it runs? Explain How to make it secure?

What are zombie host and a reflector host?

Explain OSI Layers and Compare it with TCP/IP Stack?

Explain the use of nslookup in digital Forensic?

Which header in the email is used by a forensic investigator?

Which header is mostly forged in an email?

Which email protocol provides remote searching and filing?

Forgers use which header of email to send spam?

Explain the use of Reverse DNS?

List DNS Packet Structure?

As a Forensics Examiner how will you perform analysis

What features you will look for in a Computer Forensic e-discovery Tool?

As a Forensics Examiner which Computer Forensic Software Tools you have used?

As a Forensics Examiner what command will you use to see hidden files on Windows

As a Forensics Examiner what you think is the best Acquisition Method?

As a Forensics Examiner have you used forensic hash, what are the rules?

Explain the concept of Subscriber identity module (SIM) cards?

As a Forensics Examiner how will extract data from SIM cards?

As a Forensics Examiner what Social Media Investigation Tools you have used?

As a Forensics Examiner how will you investigate in a wireless environment?

In UNIX how to find hidden files and directories?

Explain Coercivity?

What is Hearsay evidence?

How to analyze deleted and active files? And how to include Date and Time Stamps?

Explain NTFS Architecture? What are the components?

List NTFS Boot Sector?

How to interpret NTFS Boot Sector?

What is resident attribute?

Explain types of data acquisition?

How to Zero a drive in UNIX?

How to Partition Drive in Linux?

Where you will look for hashed UNIX passwords?

As computer forensic expert what are the basic rules you follow in an investigation?

Explain various fields of /etc/shadow file?

Which file in UNIX is used to monitor each time the su command is used?

Explain the use of a NAT router?

What is Syslogd in UNIX?

Explain Distance-vector routing protocols? What methods are used by it?

When Internet Content Adaptation Protocol (ICAP) is used?

What are the steps in analysis and processing of digital images?

How will you match fingerprints in a database?

Name the components of IAFIS?

How will you protect data by providing encryption for entire volumes?

Can you securely erase hard drives?

Name some of the techniques which are used in digital image processing?

Which Hard Drive Technology is best for Database?

How will you finding vulnerabilities

Which E-mail Protocols and ports are commonly used?

Explain MBR?

How to prevent the Man-in-the-middle attacks?

What are the functions of the TRIAD?

Run Programs In The Background

UNIX Summary of Commands useful for Forensics

These Commands are referenced from UNIX Manpages.

Find

Combining the find and cpio command

Removing Cores Conditionally

Copy a tree with cpio and preserve the original owner and group information for the directories and files

Find the Hog

Searching for old files

Non Technical/Personal/HR interview: Complimentary

Bottom Line Job interview?

Interview Question?

What are your greatest strengths?

What are your greatest weaknesses?

Had you failed to do any work and regret?

Where do you see yourself five years from now?

How Will You Achieve Your Goals?

Why are you leaving Your Current position?

Why are you looking for a new job?

Why should I hire you?

Aren't you overqualified for this position?

Describe a Typical Work Week?

Are You Willing to Travel?

Describe the pace at which you work?

How Did You Handle Challenges?

How do you handle pressure? Stressful situations?

How Many Hours Do You Work?

Why are you the best person for the job?

What are you looking for in a position?

What do you know about our organization?

What are your short term goals?

What Salary are you looking for?

Tell me more about yourself.

Why did you leave your previous job?

What relevant experience do you have?

If your previous co-workers were here, what would they say about you?

Where else have you applied?

What motivates you to do a good job?

Are you good at working in a team?

Has anything ever irritated you about people you've worked with?

Is there anyone you just could not work with?

Tell me about any issues you've had with a previous boss.

Any questions?

Why did you choose this career?

What did you learn from your last job experience?

How do you keep current and informed about your job and the industries that you have worked in?

Tell me about a time when you had to plan and coordinate a project from start to finish?

What kinds of people do you have difficulties working with?

What do you want to be in 5 years?

Ideal career?

Responsibilities?

Dream job?

Skills?

What sets you apart?

If the project not gone as planned?

If unable to meet Deadlines?

Interpersonal skill?

Improve?

What do you feel has been your greatest work-related accomplishment?

Have you ever had to discipline a problem employee? If so, how did you handle it?

Why do you want this position?

Why are you the best person for this job?

What about Technical writing?

How versatile you are? Can you do other works?

How do you manage time?

How do you handle Conflicts?

What kind of supervisory skills you have?

Any Bad Situation you could not solve?

Anything else?

Digital and Computer Forensics Examiner Job Interview Questions?

Suggested Answers

What is Computer Forensics?

Computer forensics is the application of computer investigation and analysis techniques in the interests of determining potential legal evidence.

What does Computer Forensics do?[1]

Computer forensics collect, analyze and present suspect data to a court of law.

How to Perform Computer Forensics?

I perform it in a four (4) steps:
   I.   Acquisition
   II. Identification
   III. Evaluation
   IV. Presentation

What you suggest for Digital Crime Scene Investigation?

Treat every incident as if it will end up in a criminal prosecution.

What is Malware?

Malware, short for malicious software, is software used or created by hackers to disrupt computer operation, gather sensitive information, or gain access to private computer systems. While it is often software, it can also appear in the form of scripts or code.'Malware' is a general term used to refer to a variety of forms of hostile, intrusive, or annoying software.(Reference: Wikipedia)

What are the different forms of Malware have you worked with?

I.   Virus

II. Trojans

III. Worms

IV. Spyware

V.   Adware

VI. Rootkits

How to Discover, analyze, diagnose, and report on malware events?

I have used these tools:

I. Grep: It is a command line tool writer for UNIX system for searching for text.
II. AVG Antivirus: The antivirus software is use for detecting and removing malware.
III. Whois: To find the contact information for IP address
IV. IDA Pro: To commercial disassembling and debugging software.
V. hexedit: This is use for viewing and editing the raw data of a file in hex format.
VI. VMWare: To create a virtual machine
VII. FileAlyzer: File analysis tool developed by safer networking.
VIII. Helix: A live Linux for forensics analysis.
IX. Sysinternals: Manage, diagnose, troubleshoot, and monitor Windows systems

You have to Collect and preserve data using accepted forensic protocols? What are the protocols?

i.   It should be repeatable
ii. It should be defensible
iii. It should protect the data from tampering
iv. It should protect the metadata

Do you have Analytical understanding of Windows registry for forensic investigation?

It's the file that contains vital information for several aspects of a computer. It's a hierarchical database used in the Microsoft Windows family of Operating Systems to store information necessary to configure the system for one or more users, applications and hardware devices.

The registry has 2 pieces of information:
       I. System-Wide Information
      II. User Specific Information

Security Registry: \Windows\system32\config
For example HKEY_LOCAL_MACHINE (HKLM) contains system-wide hardware settings and configuration information.

Explain Cloning?

The disk-to-disk process of copying a source disk, sector-by-sector to a destination disk.

Explain disk wiping?

This will erase all data on an image drive. It overwrites each sector on the drive and truly erases the data.

What are the two general wipe options?

One-pass write and multi-pass write

What are the methods available to erase data?

The methods available to erase data are deleting the file, format a drive, and delete the partition

Explain forensic disk duplicators?

The Forensic Duplicator provides forensic (write-protected source drive) disk-to-file or disk-to-disk duplication

Define imaging?

Disk-to-file.
Copies source disk into one or more files on the destination disk.

What Compound files are you familiar with? How to Search them?

For searching I have mounted compound files.
.zip
.gzip
.gz
.rar
VHD
VMDK

Explain How a computer Boots?

Hardware needs a program to find Operatin system; it's called Bootstrap loader (E.g. BIOS – Boot Input Output System)

Bootstrap loader is responsible for locating the kernel, loading it into main memory and starting its execution.

It Runs a Power-On Self Test (POST) to check all the components.

BIOS will find the device that is bootable.

It Initializes CPU registers, device controllers and contents of the main memory and it loads the OS.

BIOS loads and executes its boot sector.

The MBR code checks the partition table for an active partition. MBR code loads that partition's boot sector, loads and executes a kernel, which continues startup.

What is a file that contains vital information for several aspects of a computer?

Windows Registry

Explain why Firewalls can be used to detect Forensic Evidence for malicious attacks?

The firewall and IDS are used to handle the network attacks, but they have many limitations, such as, it cannot protect against attacks that bypass them, not protect against internal threats, and not detect new attacks. The analysis, examination and reconstruction of an attack cannot be
Based on the firewall logs and IDS alerts.

In case of an attack on computer or network what logs you should collect?

Timestamp, intruder IP address, victim IP address/port, protocol information

Explain Distributed Denial of Service Attacks?

A Distributed Denial of Service (DDoS) attack uses many computers to launch a coordinated DoS attack against one or more targets by using client/server technology.

How to prevent a Distributed Denial of Service (DDoS) attack?

By IDIP (Intruder Detection and Isolation Protocol). It works
on the principle of Trace and Block. When an attack traverses
an IDIP-protected network, each IDIP node along the path is
responsible for auditing the connection. IDIP trace message is
sent when a sufficiently intrusive Event(s) detected to warrant a
response. It includes description of the event, including a
description of the connection used by the intruder.

How to prevent foot printing?

By using Network Address Translation.
NAT hides the footprint of the network.
Network Address Translation hides a number of hosts behind
a single IP address.

What is stealth rule?

It is the first rule in the Rule Base. The purpose of this is to
prevent traffic from directly accessing the firewall itself.

What is Full disk encryption?

Full disk encryption (FDE) is when a whole hard drive or the
entirety of a particular volume has been encrypted.

How to detecte illegal software distribution?

I will use a packet sniffer.

It is a software application that uses a network adapter card in
promiscuous mode to capture all network packets.

How many ports are in TCP/IP Protocol Suite

TCP/IP Protocol Suite TCP/IP has 65535 ports available

What is brute force attacks and how to prevent it?

The brute force attack is a method of obtaining a user's
authentication credentials.
Brute force attacks are defined by the repeated attempts to
connect to the firewall, by testing all password combinations
possible.
I Enable protection from force attacks on Firewall.
I will block IP addresses permanently that are in
/var/log/messages for failed login attempts.

What kind of IP is assigned to ISP dial up accounts and how to
track it?

"Dynamic" IP addresses are temporarily assigned from a pool
of available addresses registered to an ISP when a user begins
an online session so a device's IP address may vary from one
logon session to the next. ISPs may log the date, time, account
user information, and ANI (Automatic Number Identification)
or caller line identification at the time of connection.

What is Triage?

Categorize, prioritize and assign events and incidents of
computer security incidents

Explain Secure Hash Algorithm?

It's a Cryptographic hash functions commonly used in Digital Forensic. It was Developed by NIST, specified in the Secure Hash Standard (SHS, FIPS Pub 180), 1993
SHA is specified as the hash algorithm in the Digital Signature Standard (DSS), NIST.
Message is processed in 512-bit blocks sequentially.
Message digest is 160 bits,

How to store the entire partition?

I have used "dd" command to make a bit-by-bit copy of a hard drive. dd reads every single block, including any blocks which the OS avoids.

I have used to duplicate a HDD sdc2 to sdd2.
Code:
```
dd if=/dev/sdc2 of=/dev/sdd2 bs=4096 conv=notrunc,
noerror
```

Here is a syntax as referenced from man page:
NAME
     dd - convert and copy a file

SYNOPSIS
     /usr/bin/dd [operand=value]...

DESCRIPTION
     The dd utility copies the specified input file to the specified output
     With possible conversions. The standard input and output are used by
     Default. The input and output block sizes may be specified to take

Advantage of raw physical I/O. Sizes are specified in bytes; a   number

May end with k, b, or w to specify multiplication by 1024, 512, or 2,

Respectively. Numbers may also be separated by x to indicate multipli-

Cation.

How to perform Forensic log parsing of IIS or a web hack?

How to see what ip addresses attempted to log into your FTP site?

Microsoft's Log Parser utility

Explain your experience using the inode structure?

An inode is a data structure in UNIX operating systems that contains important information pertaining to files within a file system.

It has important forensic information contained in the inode
  I. Inode number
  II. Mode information to discern file type and also for the stat C function
  III. Number of links to the file
  IV. UID of the owner
  V. Group ID (GID) of the owner
  VI. Size of the file
  VII. Actual number of blocks that the file uses
  VIII. Time last modified
  IX. Time last accessed
  X. Time last changed

I have been using the `ls -i` command, to view the inumber next to the file name.

Explain The Sleuth Kit?

The Sleuth Kit (TSK) is a tool kit written by Brian Carrier containing open source
Forensic analysis tools and TSK provides tools that function at five layers:
I.   File System Layer (information about the file system)
II. Content Layer Tools (blocks, block size)
III. Meta data (deals with data section of block owned by inode)
IV. Human Interface Layer (File and directory entries)
V.   Media Management (partition)

How to ensure time synchronization on Logs?

All security related forensic analysis requires that all data captured be time-stamped using a common reference time synchronization standard.
NTP provides a means to ensure that the system clocks and time stamps of the many computers in a network are well synchronized. The Network Time Protocol (NTP) is a protocol for synchronizing the clocks of computer systems over packet-switched, variable-latency data networks to a common time base (usually UTC, or also known as GMT – Coordinated Universal Time). NTP uses UDP port 123 as its transport layer.

How determine the integrity of a file or a disk on Linux?

By md5sum - compute and check MD5 message digest

SYNOPSIS

md5sum [OPTION] [FILE]...
md5sum [OPTION] --check [FILE]
DESCRIPTION
Print or check MD5 (128-bit) checksums.
With no FILE, or when FILE is -, read standard input.
It checks the integrity of a file by providing a 128 bit digital signature.

Can you explain the difference between primary & secondary transfers?

1. **Primary Transfer A -> B**
2. **Secondary Transfer A -> B -> C**

As a Digital Forensics Investigator what you think affects transfer?

I. **Properties of article, Mechanical interaction of bodies via surfaces**
II. **Number of contacts Size (area) of contact dependent on forces, materials, geometry, temperature**
III. **Pressure of contact, weight of the object divided by the area**
IV. **Duration of contact, time**

What is ISFA Code of Ethics?

Maintain honesty, integrity, objectivity and impartiality and Carry out all duties in a professional manner.

Explain Diffie-Hellman Encryption Algorithms?

Diffie and Hellman introduced the concept of public-key cryptography.
Diffie-Hellman is an asymmetric key algorithm used for public key cryptography and IPSec, it is also used for SSL, SSH, PGP and other PKI systems.
A Diffie-Hellman key consists of four values: p, a large prime, g, and a primitive
Element under mod p, d, a random number between 1 and p-2, and e, which is gd mod p.
Only d, the decryption key, is kept secret.

What authority IRT - Leader has?

IRT Leader has the authority of an executive during an incident.
The team leader is responsible for the initiation of an IRT investigation and IRT activities performed in support of the investigation, Conduct IRT meetings, and Coordinate IRT investigation.

Explain the use of a honey pot in Forensic?

It's a fake system that is used for fooling the attackers. It's used to

Detect automated probes, attacks, Capture tools, new worms, etc.

Explain the Foreign Intelligence Surveillance Act of 1978? How it relates to forensic?

Foreign Intelligence Surveillance Act 1978 Title III (Wiretap Statue) regulates ordinary law enforcement surveillance and has provided special procedures for conducting electronic surveillance.

It regulates government's collection of "foreign intelligence" for the purpose of counterintelligence. The Act provides for surveillance of American citizens and others for whom the court determines that there is probable cause that they are agents of a foreign power. Regulates Electronic eavesdropping and wiretapping.

The Counterfeit Access Device and Computer Fraud and Abuse Act of 1986 Prohibits what?

I. "Access[ing] a protected computer without authorization" so as to perpetuate a fraud and "obtain anything of value";
II. Knowingly "caus[ing] the transmission of a program, information, code or command" So as to intentionally cause damage to a protected computer;
III. Accessing a protected computer without authorization, in a manner that causes "damage" to the computer; or
IV. Causing damage to a protected computer through the unauthorized transmission of computer passwords.

What is Stored Communications Act?

Stored Communications Act or "SCA," specifically governs stored communications and stored subscriber identifying data and transactional data.

Designed to protect the privacy of electronic records and communications stored with third parties :

  I. Provider of electronic communication service to the public (ECS)
  II. Provider of remote computing service to the public (RCS)

What is Computer Fraud and Abuse Act? How it affects Forensic?

Computer Fraud and Abuse Act (CFAA, 1986)
Title 18 U.S. Code 1030, Computer Fraud and Abuse Act (as amended in 1996) States that unauthorized access to a "Federal interest computer" is a felony and it Prescribes penalties for violation such as access, alter, damage, or destroy information on a computer without authorization.

The Computer Fraud and Abuse Act applies to :

  I. Government computers
  II. Financial computers systems
  III. Medical computers systems
  IV. Interstate commerce computers systems
  V. computers systems on the internet

What is USA PATRIOT Act? Whats for Forensic investigation?

President Bush signed the USA Patriot Act into law On October 26, 2001.

It means Uniting and Strengthening America by Providing Appropriate Tools Required to Intercept and Obstruct Terrorism Act of 2001.

It has allowed computer forensic investigation to use Internet monitoring system called "Carnivore" for access to online, e-mail activities of suspect criminals. The government can monitor online activity without any court order.

Explain File Slack? What Forensic information you can gather from it?

File Slack is the unused space in the last cluster occupied by a file and it contains leftovers of older files, Passwords etc.

Explain RAM Slack? What Forensic information you can gather from it?

RAM Slack is the unfilled area in the last sector. OS writes random data from memory (RAM) to this area so the Data collected for slack can also be a confidential data.

What is MS Windows swap file? What Forensic information you can gather from it?

A swap file or page file is an area on the hard drive used for temporary storage of information. Swap files are used as if it were random access memory (RAM) and data is transparently stored within the Windows swap file without the knowledge Of the computer user. It contains e-mail messages, Internet browsing activity, database entries, and Windows work sessions. By default the swap files are hidden.
In Windows NT, 2000, XP, Vista, and 7 Swap file name is PAGEFILE.SYS

How to prevent unauthorized access to the sensitive data stored on your computer?

I. By encrypting data at rest by tools like CRU Encryption dataport V Plus
II. Tightly controlling data access

Explain Triple Data Encryption Algorithm?

As the name suggests Triple Data Encryption Applies the DES cipher algorithm three time to each data block to increase the key size as lisred below:

$$C = Encrypt(K1, Decrypt(K2, Encrypt(K3, P)))$$

What do forensic audit use?

It commonly uses system tables, memory segments, all the system logs,
Error logs, User logs, event logs

What data must be logged for the events?

I. Time and date of activities

II. User ID

III. ID of local terminal or remote computer

IV. System job number and the process number

V. Error conditions such as failed attempts at executing a task

As a first responder how, why and when to collect evidence in the clipboard ?

I will make sure to retrieve the contents of the Clipboard, using pclip.exe. The subject machine may have evidence in the clipboard if the machine has not been restarted.

Important items are stored on the Clipboard, including file contents or passwords.

Computer must be left on, the user should not log out, and nothing should be added to the Clipboard to replace what was put there, the data remains on the Clipboard.

What is volatile evidence and how to collect volatile live evidence?

Its active system processes and network data that may be lost in the process of turning off a computer. Microsoft has created Computer Online Forensic Evidence Extractor .

Can you check evidence that keeps changing? What are the Guidelines for Evidence

Collection and Archiving? Explain the order of Volatility.

I will check registers, cache, routing tables, ARP cache, process tables, and kernel statistics and modules.

First item of volatile data that should be collected on a live system is the contents of physical memory, commonly referred to as RAM.

Guidelines for Evidence Collection and Archiving RFC 3227 has a different order of volatility as follows: Registers, cache; Routing table, arp cache, process table, kernel statistics, memory; Temporary file systems; Disk; Remote logging and monitoring data that is relevant to the system in question;Physical configuration, network topology; Archival media.

What is the first rule in digital forensics?

Preserve the original evidence

What have you done in forensic first stages of an investigation?

I had created a basic investigation plan:

I. I had acquired the evidence by using evidence collections tools such as:
  i. Sexual Assault Kits
  ii. DNA and Trace Evidence Collection Kits
  iii. Blood & Urine Collection Kits
  iv. Specimen Collection Kits

II. I had completed an evidence form and established a chain of custody

III. I had transported the evidence to a computer forensics lab

IV. I had secured the evidence in an approved secure container

V. I had prepared a forensics workstation

VI. I had obtained the evidence from the secure container

VII. I had made a forensic copy of the evidence

VIII. I had returned the evidence to the secure container

IX. I had processed the copied evidence with computer forensics tools such as :

       i. Disk imaging software
      ii. Hashing tools compare original hard disks to copies.
     iii. File recovery programs to search for and restore files.

What are the two tests for digital evidence to survive in a court of law?

    I. Authenticity
    II. Reliability

Do you have any experience in bypassing Windows security?

Yes,

If you give me a system with access to its console, I can modify the BIOS and reboot the system from another hard drive with a different OS and access NTFS or FAT files.

What are the requirements for a forensic Bootable Compact Disc?

I. Forensic Bootable Compact Disc should boot a system into an operating system that can support examination of the media attached to the booted suspect's system;

II. In booting the system, Forensic Bootable Compact Disc should should not modify any of the media on the suspect's computer;

III. Forensic Bootable Compact Disc should provide an environment in which media attached to the system can be examined or imaged without causing any modification of the attached media suspect's computer;

IV. Forensic Bootable Compact Disc must be able to support the drivers necessary to access the media attached to the system so that it can be examined and imaged accurately suspect's computer;

V. Forensic Bootable Compact Disc should provide a way for data to be copied from the suspect's computer.

Name a forensic operating system?

Linux Ubuntu

What can you do to disable passwords on the BIOS?

Remove CMOS battery

Is it possible to recover files deleted from trashcan? How?

Yes.

Windows changes one character in the file table to mark the hard drive space as being available for use so by starting an undelete process before Windows overwrites that part of hard disk with new files, it can be recovered.

Panda Recovery
TOKIWA Data Recovery
Undelete Plus

How to find users web activity on internet explorer?

I. history files in Internet Explorer
II. index.dat file
III. Content.IE5
IV. History.IE5
V. cookie files for IE

Which tools have you used for the collection of evidence?

I. Encase

II. Forensic Toolkit (FTK)

III. Sleuth Kit (TSK)

IV. Autopsy Forensic browser

Which Key loggers have you worked with?

I. Badtrans
II. Magic Lantern/Carnivore
III. Spytech Spy Agent Stealth Edition
IV. Staff Cop Standard
V. Spector Pro
VI. Stealth Keylogger
VII. SoftActivity Keylogger
VIII. eBlaster
IX. Elite Keylogger

What to compare between clone and the source drive?

Compare the MD5 or SHA1 hash between the clone and the source drive

Is it possible to detect and prevent Key loggers?

Yes.

I have used:
  I.   Anti-Virus
  II. Spyware & Firewalls
  III. Automatic Form Fillers
  IV. Alternative Keyboard Layouts
  V.   Onscreen Keyboards

What is Keystroke logging?

It's a tool that captures every key depression on the computer.

What is Rootkit?

It's a tool that provides Privileged access to a computer.

How to Detect Rootkits?

Use of Host Based Intrusion Detection System (IDS)
Tripwire
Advanced Intrusion Detection Environment (AIDE)
Chkrootkit

Which binaries are changed by lrk4?

login – this signs a user onto the system
chfn – used to change finger information

chsh – used to change login shell
passwd – updates a user's authentication token

Explain Hardware Keylogger?

It's a small cylindrical device attached to the end of the keyboard cable and then plugged into the back of your computer to record all of the data typed into the computer.

Hardware Keylogger types?

PS/2
USB
Keyboard Module
Mini-/ PCI card

Name a few Keyloggers?

Big ones
KeyDemon
KeeLog
KeyCarbon
KeyCobra
KeyLlama
KEYKatcher
KeyGhost
KeyShark

What is required for submitting forensic evidence in a testimony?

Forensic sciences are useful tool but many forensic disciplines apply techniques and methods that have not been scientifically validated. It should be validated before submitting. Validation refers to the process of determining that a scientific method is robust, reliable and reproducible.

What are the classes of computer forensics tools?

Disk imaging products, write blockers, and selected suites of tools.

What are the three forms Challenges to the authenticity of computer records can take?

I. Parties may challenge the authenticity of both computer-generated and computer-stored records by questioning whether the records were altered, manipulated, or damaged after they were created.

II. Parties may question the authenticity of computer-generated records by challenging the reliability of the computer program that generated the records.

III. Parties may challenge the authenticity of computer-stored records by questioning the identity of their author.

What you can see in the IDS logs?

Intrusion detection system (IDS) logs can contain actual packets seen on the network.

Name a few intrusion detection systems?

I. Cisco Systems' Secure IDS
II. Enterasys Networks' Dragon
III. Internet Security Systems' Black ICE
IV. Snort
V. Symantec Net Prowler

What is foot printing? What is port scanning?

Foot printing is the process of accumulating data regarding a specific network.

The purpose of foot printing is to create a map of the network to determine what operating systems, applications and address ranges are being utilized, and to identify any accessible open ports. The hacker attempts to find open ports on the target system.

Foot printing is the first logical step in any attacker's preparation before the actual hack.

Because security holes are dependent on OS version, it can easily determine which exploit to use on your network.

A hacker collects information on the network services on a target network via Port scanning.

What is Penetration Testing?

Targeting flaws and weaknesses that could be hacked and exploited by a malicious hacker

Explain Rules of evidence?

Rules of evidence govern whether, when, how, and for what purpose, proof of a legal case may be placed before a trier of fact for consideration.

How you can show that the evidence was not tampered?

Generate MD5 hash of the evidence

What is Deposition?

It's a Pre-Trial discovery.
Deposition is - "The testimony of a witness taken upon oral question or written .A pretrial discovery device by which one party (through his or her attorney) asks oral questions of the other party or of a witness for the other party.

Explain what you know about SMTP?

SMTP stands for Simple Mail Transport Protocol.
It is the method that computers connected to the Internet use to send email.
SMTP transactions typically have 4 parts:
HELO, where the computers talking identify themselves
MAIL FROM, the envelope sender of the message is given
RCPT TO, the address or addresses that the message will be sent to
DATA, the actual message (which also has all the message headers, including from: and to :)

Why to use Reverse DNS?

Reverse DNS is used to verify that the mail server is who it says it is.

Name most common email protocols?

The three most common email protocols are POP, IMAP and MAPI

How to identify a TCP connection? List some common ports?

TCP connection is identified by: srce IP addr, srce port, dest IP addr, dest port

Port	Protocol	Description
23	Telnet	Terminal Emulation (Telephone network)

21   FTP   Allows file transfers between computers (File Transfer Protocol)

69   TFTP   Have to know what you want and where it is on the server, no directory browsing, no user authentication (Trivial File Transfer Protocol)

2049   NFS   Allows remote file systems to be mounted as local (Network File System)

25   SMTP Used to send mail between mail servers (Simple Mail Transfer Protocol)

515   LPD   Used for print sharing of network printers with TCP/IP (Line Printer Daemon)

161   SNMP   Collect and manipulates network information (Simple Network Management Protocol)

53   DNS   Resolves FQDN to IP addresses (Domain Name Service)

67   BootP Used by diskless workstations to receive boot file and other information via TFTP

546   DHCP Client

547   DHCP Server

DHCP   Assigns IP addresses to hosts from a pool. Can send IP address, Subnet mask,
Domain Name, Default Gateway, DNS IP, WINS info.
(Dynamic Host Configuration Protocol)

Explain why Host-based IDS miss DOS attacks? Whats the Solution?

Host-based IDS do not see packet headers, so they cannot detect these types of attacks.
This type of attack can be quickly identified by a network-based system looking at the packet stream in real-time.

Explain your experience with Chain of Custody?

It's a record of individuals who have had physical possession of the evidence.
This record contains:
1. Identity of the person who collected the item.
2. Time and date of collection.
3. Location where item was found.

How will you maintain an accurate and complete chain of custody?

I will limit the number of individuals handling evidence.
I will make sure that all names, identification numbers, and dates are listed on the chain-of-custody documents.
I will make sure that all evidence packaging is properly sealed and marked prior to submission.
I will obtain signed receipts upon transfer of evidence.

Do you have any experience in Identifying and Mitigating source address spoofing?

Yes.

I had used anti spoofing with uRPF Unicast Reverse Path Forwarding (uRPF) a security tool that helps mitigate source IP address spoofing by discarding IP packets that lack a verifiable IP source address in the IP routing table.

Explain Spoofing?

It's a method of attacking a network in order to gain unauthorized access.
The attacker "spoofs" the source IP address of a "trusted" IP address.
Spoofing is done by forging the source IP of packets when an intruder crafts an IP datagram with a source IP address that does not belong to them.

How to determine whether your systems might be vulnerable to denial of service (DoS) attacks? How to prevent it?

I will use:
netstat -n -p tcp
If I notice multiple SYN_RECEIVED entries, my system is vulnerable to attack.
I will Use Firewall and SynAttackProtect registry in windows.
SynAttackProtect protects the server from network Denial-Of-Service attacks.

Explain your experience with Spoofing Prevention Methods?

I have prevented the IP spoofing problem by installing a filtering router by restricting the input to external interface by not allowing a packet through if it has a source address from the internal network.

I have filtered the outgoing packets that had a source address different from internal network in order to prevent a source IP spoofing.

Also I have protected router against Denial of Service attacks
By using quos Rate Limiting
By Using Urpf to check packets that lack a verifiable source IP address
By Using Egress filtering to filter outgoing traffic from AS at edge router
By Using Ingress filtering to filter incoming traffic to ISPs at edge routers
By Using Ingress filtering to selectively filter incoming traffic to ISPs at edge and core routers reverse path forwarding
By Using Key verification to Lookup only source IP in in-AS table
By using security ACL to:

    I. Deny incoming packets when source address is allocated to your network

   II. Deny outbound packets when source address is not allocated to your network

Which tools have you used to recover files?

I have used Software tools to recover files
          I. Norton Un-erase
        II. EnCase
     III. Recuva
I have used Hardware tools to recover files
          I. Raw Disk Readers
        II. Salvation DATA

How to Delete or neutralize computer viruses?

Disable System Restore
Download OS Updates
Run a Complete Anti-Virus Scan and
    I. **Clean**: remove the infection from the file.
   II. **Quarantine**: move the file to a safe location
  III. **Delete**: Removes the file completely from the system.
Run an Anti-Malware scan with Malwarebytes

What is ARP Poisoning (Man-in-the-Middle) Attack?

ARP-Poisoning is an attack that allows an attacker to become man-in-the-middle (MITM) in a local network, the attacker can forge spoofed ICMP packets to force the host to make an ARP request. Immediately after the ICMP it sends the fake ARP reply

Thereby making all traffic between two or more hosts on the network pass through the attacker. A MITM attacker can therefore see all the traffic.

What port is for LDAP?

ldap389 tcp Lightweight Directory Access Protocol

Explain the TCP three-way handshake?

The TCP three-way handshake in Transmission Control Protocol SYN, SYN-ACK, ACK, because there are three messages transmitted by TCP to negotiate and start a TCP session between two computers.

What is black hat hacker?

Black hat hacker compromises the security of a computer system without permission from an authorized party, typically with malicious intent.

How to Detect and recover erased files?

There are tools for recovery:
For Windows:

Drivespy
Encase
Forensic Tool kit
Norton Utilities

For UNIX

The Coroner's tool kit
XWays
UDF
TASK

How to crack password protected files?

AccessData Password Recovery Toolkit (PRTK) can be used to crack it.

Explain your experience with Metadata?

It is described as "data about data" and from a digital forensics perspective, metadata is also defined as: evidence, typically stored electronically, that
Describes the characteristics, origins, usage and validity of
Other electronic evidence.

How to perform Metadata extraction and analysis?

There are many computer forensic uses of
Metadata as Metadata is data that describes data.
Metadata extraction tools can be used to analyze it:

Exif, WV, libextractor, bulk_extractor

Explain the architecture of Metadata extraction Tools?

It has adapters and each adapter is registered in the system (config.xml) that is
Responsible for parsing a specific input file type. Each adapter
Must extend the Data Adapter class, which defines several
Methods:

  I. accepts File(File)

II. adapt(File, Data Adapter)
III. getOutputType()
IV. getInputType()

How to acquire a forensically protected disk image?

By Ultra Kit, attach it to the source drive, attach your target drive to the Write Enabled Ultra Block-IDE, and acquire a forensically protected disk image.

Also by using <u>F</u>orensic <u>R</u>ecovery of <u>E</u>vidence <u>D</u>evice: We can remove the hard drive(s) from the suspect system and plug them into FRED and acquire the digital evidence.

Have you worked with Hachoir?

Hachoir is a generic framework for binary file manipulation.

It's written in Python, its operating system independent.
It has many text/graphic users that allows to view and edit a binary
Stream field by field.

It supports more than sixty file formats:

Archives: bzip2, gzip, zip, tar
Audio: MP3, WAV, Sun/NeXT audio, OGG, MIDI,
AIFF, AIFC, RA
Video: WMV video, AVI, MKV, MOV, Ogg/Theora,
RM
Image: BMP, CUR, EMF, ICO, GIF, JPEG, PCX,
PNG, TGA, TIFF, WMF, XCF
Program: EXE
Misc: Torrent

EnCase uses which two methods for identifying file types?

    I. File Extensions
   II. File Signatures

How proficient are you in open source forensic tools?

I have used Sleuth Kit (TSK) open source digital investigation
Tools and it runs on Windows and UNIX systems. I have used
it to
Analyze NTFS, FAT, HFS+, Ext2, Ext3, UFS1, and UFS2
File systems and several volume system types

It has C library and a collection of command line tools such as:
    I. blkcat: To display the contents of file system data unit
       in a disk image
   II. blkls: to output the contents of unallocated data blocks
       by default
  III. blkcalc: It converts between unallocated disk unit
       numbers and regular disk unit numbers
  IV. ffind: To find the name of the file or directory using a
       given inode
   V. fls: To list file and directory names in a disk image

Explain Host Protected Area? How to check it?

The Host Protected Area (HPA) is a reserved area on a Hard
Disk Drive (HDD) to store information in such a way that it
cannot be easily modified, changed, or accessed by the user,
BIOS, or the OS.

disk stat utility which is part of Brian Carrier's The Sleuth Kit can be used to check it.

What is DCO?

An additional hidden area on many of today's HDDs is the Device Configuration Overlay (DCO). The DCO allows system vendors to purchase HDDs from different manufacturers with potentially different sizes, and then configure all HDDs to have the same number of sectors.

Which Anti Forensic tool can modify Timestamps?

Timestomp has the ability to modify timestamp values on an NTFS system.

What is the length of a Dword?

32 bits (4 bytes)

What is found in EnCase Case File?

Pointers to evidence files
Signature analysis results
Search results

What are the various .ini Files in EnCase?

EnCase uses .ini located in the config folder.
.INI files store global changes and settings to the EnCase environment.
The global environment dictates information/tools available for all cases.
Viewers.ini

Database information regarding the viewers that EnCase can use when viewing data.
SecurityIDs.ini
Stores the database of user IDs and usernames
Keywords.ini
Search terms are stored

How to take a memory dump with Knoppix-STD tools?

By using memfetch, it forces a memory dump.

How to check a UNIX system for a buffer overflow attack?

`/var/adm/messages` logs overflow attempt

What are the components of Encase Evidence file?

The header, checksum and data blocks

Explain Zero day attacks?

It is named zero days because it occurs before the first day the vulnerability is known. Attackers look for problem before a patch has been created.

List the rules of evidence?

    I. Admissible
   II. Authentic
  III. Complete
  IV. Reliable
   V. Believable

How to examine which hosts has been connected to by Telnet?

HKEY_CURRENT_USER\Software\Microsoft\Telnet

How to see Forensic Evidence for malicious attacks on a Firewall?

Show logging command with keywords to find relevant log messages

List Forensic Artifacts in a Browser?

Web browser cache, cookies, favorites, history, auto complete information, login data,
Shortcuts, web data, profile

Explain PPM – Probabilistic Packet Marking?

Probabilistically mark each packet with partial path info using some coding algorithms to reveal internal network information to end-hosts

Explain steganography?

Hide important data inside file, serial number or watermark into a data file.

Which ports used by Windows are Most Vulnerable?

The ports used by Windows NetBIOS over TCP/IP are among the most vulnerable to hackers.

Which ports NetBIOS uses over TCP?

NetBIOS session traffic over TCP port 139
NetBIOS name management traffic over UDP port 137
NetBIOS datagram traffic over UDP port 138

Which are popular Email Ports?

POP3 - port 110
IMAP - port 143
SMTP - port 25
HTTP - port 80
Secure SMTP (SSMTP) - port 465
Secure IMAP (IMAP4-SSL) - port 585
IMAP4 over SSL (IMAPS) - port 993
Secure POP3 (SSL-POP) - port 995

Name 2 most used cryptographic hash functions?

MD5 and SHA-1.

What is FTP, In terms of security what makes it difficult to control the File Transfer Protocol (FTP) via a firewall rule set or packet filter?

FTP is a TCP based service exclusively. There are two channels; one for commands and one for data .There is no UDP component to FTP. FTP is an unusual service in that it utilizes two ports, a 'data' port and a 'command' port (also known as the control port). Traditionally these are port 21 for the command port and port 20 for the data port. The confusion begins however, when we find that depending on the mode, the data port is not always on port 20.

Explain various components of Disks?

Sector
Track
Cylinder
Head
Platter

The Disk Platter is the circular *DISK* on which the magnetic data is stored
The platter is spun at incredible speeds by the central spindle.

The Drive Head read and write information bits to and from the magnetic domains

The Actuator Arm assembly which holds the heads and make sure that they are positioned
 Over the correct disk track. Drive head will pick up far more data per second from a platter
Which spins at 15000 Rotations per Minute (RPM) than one with 750 RPM?

What is Average Latency of a drive?

This is the time taken for the platter to undergo half a disk rotation.

What is Average Seek Time of a drive?

For I/O requests the average seek time is time taken for the head to travel half way across the disk.

Explain the I/O Data Path?

Path of the data I/O
1. Starts at the application
2. Goes to the storage system
3. Returns back to the application

I trace the I/O data path from application to spindle, I/O Journey starts and ends at the application as:

App ⇔HOST/HBA⇔SAN Switch/Director ⇔Storage Array

Also I will take *IN-DEPTH LOOK AT THE I/O DATA* Inside the Storage Array:

Storage Array ⇔Array Port ⇔CHP⇔Cache⇔ACP⇔Disk (Hard disk drive consists of a spindle on which the platters spin at a constant RPM while the read-write heads locate and exchange data)

Explain your experience with DNS, and what you did to make it secure?

The Domain Name System (DNS) is used for resolving host names into Internet Protocol (IP) addresses. Insecure underlying protocols and lack of authentication and integrity checking of the information within the DNS threatens the proper functionality of the DNS. That's why they came up with DNSSEC.DNSSEC is an addition to the Domain Name System (DNS) protocols.DNSSEC allows for a DNS zone and all the records in the zone to be cryptographically signed.

How does DNSSec provide greater security?

It supports cryptographically signed zones for greater trust
across the domain name
System.

What are the tasks associated with DNSSEC?

Doing DNSSEC involves two tasks:

1) Cryptographically signing authoritative DNS
records, and

2) Validating those signatures on recursive resolvers.

What is SMTP, Which port it runs? Explain How to make it secure?

Simple Mail Transfer Protocol (SMTP) is an Internet standard
for electronic mail (e-mail) transmission across Internet
Protocol (IP) networks. Port 25.

To Make it secure I had used SMTP Security Options:

Reject mail if sender address is from an invalid domain
Authenticated senders must use valid sender address
Senders from local domains must authenticate to send email
Hide IP addresses from email headers

What are zombie host and a reflector host?

Hosts that are running attack tools are known as zombies.
Reflector is an uncompromised host that cooperates with the
attack.

Explain OSI Layers and Compare it with TCP/IP Stack?

OSI N0.	OSI Layer Name	TCP/IP No.	TCP/IP Layer Name	Encapsulation Units	TCP/IP Protocols
7	Application	4	Application	data	FTP, HTTP, POP3, IMAP, telnet, SMTP, DNS, TFTP
6	Presentation			data	
5	Session			data	
4	Transport	3	Transport	segments	TCP, UDP
3	Network	2	Internet	packets	IP
2	Data Link	1	Network	frames	

1	Physical		Access	bits		

Explain the use of nslookup in digital Forensic?

nslookup is a network administration command-line tool available for many computer operating systems for querying the Domain Name System (DNS) to obtain domain name or IP address mapping or for any other specific DNS record.

Which header in the email is used by a forensic investigator?

The received is the most important and most reliable part of the email header.

Which header is mostly forged in an email?

From header displays who the message is from, and it be easily forged and can be the least reliable.

Which email protocol provides remote searching and filing?

IMAP enables email messages to remain on the email server, and allows remote searching and filing.

Forgers use which header of email to send spam?

Received: from source

Explain the use of Reverse DNS?

Reverse DNS is IP address to domain name mapping so its used in tracking where a web-site visitor came from, or where an e-mail message originated.

List DNS Packet Structure?

All DNS packets have a structure as:
Header
Question
Answer
Authority
Additional

As a Forensics Examiner how will you perform analysis

I.   **I will acquire the Data**

II. **I will authenticate Data**

III. **Imaging of Evidence Drive:** ensure that the evidence data is not destroyed

IV. **Wiping Analysis Drive**

V.   **Restoring**

What features you will look for in a Computer Forensic e-discovery Tool?

    I.   **Forensic Tools should support major Operating Systems**
   II.   **Forensic Tools should support most File System types**
  III.   **Forensic Tools Features**
  IV.   **Forensic Tools Venders Reputation**
   V.   **Forensic Tools Acceptance**
  VI.   **Forensic Tools Validation**

As a Forensics Examiner which Computer Forensic Software Tools you have used?

For Windows OS:
    I.   **EnCase computer forensics software and hardware**
   II.   **Forensic Toolkit, or FTK, computer forensics software made by AccessData**
  III.   **ProDiscover commercial forensic tool made by Technology Pathways**
  IV.   **OSForensics Software by PassMark digital investigation tool**

For Linux OS:
    I.   **Sleuth Kit and Autopsy digital forensics tools**
   II.   **Helix tool for digital forensics Incident Response & Forensics tools**

III. Knoppix STD computer forensics / incident response tools
IV. SMART for Data Forensics, Electronic Discovery

As a Forensics Examiner what command will you use to see hidden files on Windows.

I. dir /r

II. dir /ah

III. dir /ah-d

IV. attrib

As a Forensics Examiner what you think is the best Acquisition Method?

I. Bit-stream disk-to-image file, forensic copy

II. Bit-stream disk-to-disk, Bit-by-bit copy of the original

III. Logical disk-to-disk or disk-to-disk data

IV. Sparse data copy of a file or folder

As a Forensics Examiner have you used forensic hash, what are the rules?

A forensic hash is a form of a checksum.
A checksum is a mathematical calculation
I have used "Hash" values for the examination, discovery and

Authentication of electronic evidence.
I have used these three rules for forensic hashes:

    I. Eleven with hash value, its no easy to find the file or device

    From which it was generated

    II. No two hash values can be the same

    III. If anything changes in the file or device, the hash value must

    Change

Explain the concept of Subscriber identity module (SIM) cards?

    I. SIM is subscriber identity module or subscriber identification module (SIM)

    II. SIM is an integrated circuit chip found most commonly in GSM devices

    III. It securely stores the international mobile subscriber identity (IMSI)

    IV. GSM carriers put customer information on a removable SIM card.

    V. Microprocessor and from 16 KB to 1 GB EEPROM

As a Forensics Examiner how will extract data from SIM cards?

I will use a card reader to extract the data from SIM cards.

Tools:

    I. XRY Physical

    II. UFED Physical

    III. SIM Id cloning

As a Forensics Examiner what Social Media Investigation Tools you have used?

I. **Capture Tools: capture social media content and migrate to other formats**
II. **Mapping tools: Use visualizer generate animated maps of the relationships**
III. **Investigation tools: platform specific application programming interfaces (APIs) to pull content**
IV. **Mobile Devices social media**

As a Forensics Examiner how will you investigate in a wireless environment?

I. I will obtain a search warrant.
II. I will detect & identify all the wireless devices& connections.
III. I will document and maintain chain of custody.
IV. I will determine wireless field's strength, map wireless zones and hot spots.
V. I will connect to the wireless network.
VI. I will Acquire and analyze data.
VII. I will generate a report.

In UNIX how to find hidden files and directories?

```
I will use find - search for files in a directory
hierarchy
```

SYNOPSIS

```
    find [-H] [-L] [-P] [path...] [expression]
-type c
```

File is of type c:

b   block (buffered) special

c   character (unbuffered) special

d   directory

p   named pipe (FIFO)

f   regular file

l   symbolic link; this is never true if the -L
option or the

-follow option is in effect, unless the
symbolic link is

broken. If you want to search for symbolic
links when -L

is in effect, use -xtype.

s	socket
D	door (Solaris)

find . –type d –name ".*"–print0 | cat –a

Explain Coercivity?

Coercivity of magnetic media defines the magnetic field necessary to reduce a magnetically saturated material's magnetization to zero. High coercivity stripes last longer and can store data for a long period.

What is Hearsay evidence?

Hearsay testimony is secondhand evidence; it is not what the witness knows personally, but what someone else told him or her.

How to analyze deleted and active files? And how to include Date and Time Stamps?

I have used WinHex, a powerful application as an advanced hex editor and file-viewer, a tool for data analysis, editing, and recovery, a data wiping tool, and a forensics tool used for evidence gathering and IT security.

I have used Start Center dialog window and it's File Recovery with the Directory Browser tools, Deleted files and directories that are listed in the directory browser can be recovered easily and selectively with the directory browser's context menu.

It has its own Time Zone Concept, X-Ways Forensics employs its own, not Windows' logic for converting UTC to local file times. It displays timestamps independently of the time zone selected in the examiner's system's Control Panel.

Explain NTFS Architecture? What are the components?

It Stands for "New Technology File System". NTFS includes fault tolerance, which automatically repairs hard drive errors without displaying error messages. It also keeps detailed transaction logs, which tracks hard drive errors. NTFS allows permissions to be set for individual directories and files, supports spanning volumes, which allows directories of files to be spread across multiple hard drives.

Jump Instruction first three bytes are often called the Jump Instruction

Here is the NTFS components used in forensic:

Component	Component Description
Hard disk	contains one or more partitions.
Boot sector	Bootable partition that stores information about the layout of the volume and the file system structures, as well as the boot code that loads Ntdlr.
Master Boot Record	Contains executable code that the system BIOS loads into memory. The code scans the MBR to find the partition table to determine which partition is the active, or bootable, partition.
Ntldlr.dll	Switches the CPU to protected mode, starts the file system, and then reads the contents of the Boot.ini file. This information determines the startup options and initial boot menu selections.
Ntfs.sys	System file driver for NTFS.

Ntoskrnl.exe Extracts information about which system device drivers to load and the load order.

Kernel mode the processing mode that allows code to have direct access to all hardware and memory in the system.

User mode   the processing mode in which applications runs.

List NTFS Boot Sector?

I.	0x00	3B	Jump Instruction
II.	0x03	8B	OEM ID
III.	0x0B	25B	BPB
IV.	0x24	48B	Extended BPB
V.	0x54	426B	Bootstrap Code.
VI.	0x1FE	2B	End of Sector Marker

How to interpret NTFS Boot Sector?

By WinHex

What is resident attribute?

An attribute defines a file. An attribute that is guaranteed to always be present in the
MFT File Record because of a defined size is called a Resident Attribute.

Explain types of data acquisition?

I. Static acquisition
II. Live acquisition

How to Zero a drive in UNIX?

dd if=/dev/zero of=/dev/sdb

How to Partition Drive in Linux?

fdisk /dev/sdb

Where you will look for hashed UNIX passwords?

/etc/shadow

As computer forensic expert what are the basic rules you follow in an investigation?

  I.   Collection & Preservation of evidence
  II. Prevention of contamination of evidence, protective equipment
 III. Extraction and preservation of evidence
 IV. Accountability of evidence
  V. Limited interference of the crime scene on normal life
 VI. Ethics of investigation, good ETHICAL and moral character

Explain various fields of /etc/shadow file?

Shadow file format

kdp:fq5oelsPMDiG.:10078:0:99999:9:::

   I. username

   II. encrypted password

   III. Days since Jan 1, 1970 that password was last changed

   IV. Days before password may be changed

   V. Days after which password must be changed

   VI. Days before password is to expire that user is warned

   VII. Days after password expires that account is disabled

   VIII. Days since Jan 1, 1970 that account is disabled

   IX. A reserved field

Which file in UNIX is used to monitor each time the su command is used?

/var/adm/sulog

Explain the use of a NAT router?

It translates unregistered IP addresses that reside on the private (inside) network, to registered IP addresses.

What is Syslogd in UNIX?

Syslogd provides for system logging and kernel message trapping

System logs are usually text files containing a timestamp and other information
UNIX distributions have system log daemon named "syslogd".
Explain Distance-vector routing protocols? What methods are used by it?

A distance-vector routing protocol requires that a router informs its neighbors of topology changes periodically. It uses these Methods:

I. Direction in which or interface to which a packet should be forwarded.
II. Distance from its destination.

Examples of distance-vector routing protocols include RIPv1 and RIPv2 and IGRP.

When Internet Content Adaptation Protocol (ICAP) is used?

ICAP is a protocol designed to off-load specific Internet-based content to dedicated servers, it forwards HTTP content to an AV server.

What are the steps in analysis and processing of digital images?

I will utilize software applications like FTK Imager, X-Ways Forensics, computer forensics and data recovery software for the analysis and processing of digital images.
Then I will be Imaging Digital Media

Then I will Hash the media
I will make an exact copy of the media
I will Hash the image
I will prove it is an exact copy by Comparing with hash of the original by MD5, SHA1, and SHA256.

How will you match fingerprints in a database?

I will use Automated Fingerprint Identification System (AFIS)

Name the components of IAFIS?

IAFIS consists of three integrated segments:
    I. **The Identification Tasking and Networking (ITN) segment,**
    II. **The Interstate Identification Index (III),**
    III. **Automated Fingerprint Identification System (AFIS)**

How will you protect data by providing encryption for entire volumes?

I will use Bit Locker full disk encryption

Can you securely erase hard drives?

I can use these methods for data destructions:
  I.   **Block overwrite**
  II. **Magnetic degaussing**
  III. **Physical or mechanical shredding**
  IV. **Secure Erase**

Name some of the techniques which are used in digital image processing?

  I.   Pixelation
  II. Linear filtering
  III. Principal components analysis
  IV. Independent component analysis
  V.   Hidden Markov models
  VI. Anisotropic diffusion

Which Hard Drive Technology is best for Database?

SATA configurations perform well in file server and streaming media scenarios,
While SCSI configurations work well with database applications.

Database I/O should be done to raw disk partitions or direct unbuffered I/O.

How will you finding vulnerabilities

  I.   I will research

II. I will investigate

III. I will describe

IV. I will catalog

Which E-mail Protocols and ports are commonly used?

     I. POP3: Port 110, receiving e-mail
    II. SMTP: Port 25, sending e-mail
   III. IMAP: Port 143 , stores email

Explain MBR?

Master Boot Record, a small program that is executed when a computer boots up.
The MBR is sector 0, and the first partition usually starts at sector 63.

How to prevent the Man-in-the-middle attacks?

By cryptographic protocols
What are the functions of the TRIAD?

   I. Vulnerability assessment & risk management
  II. Network intrusion detection
 III. Incident response computer investigations.

UNIX Fundamental/ Commands for Forensic Analysts

LOGIN:

Telnet is a TCP/IP terminal emulation protocol which enables **remote login(s)** Telnet is also a UNIX command which starts the telnet program on a UNIX computer.

telnet

Uses telnet protocol to connect to another remote computer.

Syntax

telnet [-8] [-E] [-L] [-c] [-d] [-r] [-e escape_char] [-l user] [-n file] [host [port]]

Using telnet

telnet xxx.xxx.xxx

Where **xxx.xxx.xxx** is site you are trying to connect to.

telnet Servername

Shell login

ssh - OpenSSH SSH client (remote login program)
EXAMPLES
SYNOPSIS
ssh [-l login_name] hostname | user@hostname [command]

For an interactive session at the command prompt shell the syntax is:

ssh *user@host*

user

      Your teaching domain Unix login name.

host

      The machine to login to.

Manual command

 man man

This is help command, and use it with man in conjunction with any unix command to learn more about that command for example.

man cat will explain about the cat command and how you can use it.

Data Migration

Cpio
To Copy files from one directory tree to another use cpio

To copy the files of the present directory, and sub-directories to a new directory called newdir:

find . -depth -print0 | cpio --null -pvd newdir

cd /source/directory/

find . -depth -print | cpio -pduvm /destination/directory

tar

tar command is useful for storing a number of files in one file ,traditionally on a magnetic tape, but it can be done on another file.

To copy :

cd /<source directory>

tar -cf - * | (cd /<target directory>;tar -xf -)

Also Creating a new directory called destdir for the files to be copied into

$ tar cpf - . | (mkdir /tmp/destdir ; cd /tmp/destdir; tar xvpf -)

Global Substitution:

To apply a substitution to every occurrence in every line, add the operator g to the end.

Simple substitution of word old to new in a file named test

sed 's/old/new/g' test

Search:

Examples grep 'testfile1' /etc/passwd

This command will searche for all occurrences of the text string 'testfile1' within the "/etc/passwd" file. It will find and print (on the screen) all of the lines in this file that contain the text string 'testfile1', including lines that contain usernames like "testfile1" and also "nltestfile1".

grep 'testfile1' *

This command searches for all occurrences of the text string 'testfile1' within all files of the current directory.

Printing

```
lp - print files
```

SYNOPSIS

```
      lp  [  -E  ]  [ -U username ] [ -c ] [ -d
destination[/instance] ] [ -h
      hostname[:port] ] [ -m ] [ -n num-copies ] [ -o
option[=value] ]          [  -q
```

```
        priority ] [ -s ] [ -t title ] [ -H handling ] [
-P page-list ] [ -- ]
        [ file(s) ]
        lp [ -E ] [ -U username ] [ -c ] [ -h
hostname[:port] ] [ -i job-id ] [
        -n num-copies ] [ -o option[=value] ] [ -q
priority ] [ -t title ] [ -H
        handling ] [ -P page-list ]
```

"lp" is the command used to print files.

Examples lp /my/code

This command prints the "/my/code " file to the default printer.

Linking

ln

Creates a link to a file.

Syntax

ln [-f] [-n] [-s] existingfile newname

symbolic link, also termed a soft link, is a special kind of file that points to another file, symbolic link is a pointer or an alias to another file.

>ln -s source-file dest-file

So If we remove the file a symbolic link points to, the link remains but it points nowhere.

Hard links

A hard link is a duplicate inode .

 # ln test link

Both files have the same inode

 # ls -i test link
112192 test 112192 link

So If a file is pointed to by a hard link, it cannot be removed until the link is removed, all of the original files must be removed before the file can be removed

Making a backup copy

Its essential that you make a backup copy of any configuration file or the code that you are editing. So you can revert to the backup copy if you made a mistake.

>cp testfile1 testfile1.back

This makes a backup copy using the 'cp' command in the shell,

Erase data
dd if=/dev/zero of=/dev/123
Where /dev/123 is the name of the device to erase

The Environment variables

To get the information about the System and Environment variables

```
$ env
HOME=ex
PATH=/bin:/sbin:/usr/bin
SHELL=/bin/bash
PWD=/usr/bl/cfiles
TERM=ansi
TZ=
USER=bl
GROUP=tes
HOSTNAME=bline
```

PATH

To add a PATH variable

```
$ set PATH=$PATH:/usr/java/jdk
```

```
$ export PATH
```

This will add the path of JDK which is installed at /usr/java/jdk to the path variable

To find the path

$ which blc
 /usr/java/blc

Deletion

You may have to clear ,delete files to create space when a
folder is full.

> rm -i testfile1*

the 'rm' command deletes the files immediately
The "-i" option with the 'rm' command will prompt you for
confirmation before deleting each file. Its recommended to use
this "safety" when using 'rm' with wildcards.

Changing your password

> passwd

History

Unix keeps a record of all the commands typed and it can
replay them using the *history* command.

> To set the history variable so that the last 110 commands
> are stored

> *set history=110*

To display the history list
> *history*

Or you can see the entire file:
>cat .sh_history

Who is working

> finger   Simple list of other users.

Lists information about the user.

Syntax

finger [-b] [-f] [-h] [-i] [-l] [-m] [-p] [-q] [-s] [-w] [username]

> who   Shows who is logged onto this and other systems.

> w List of users logged into this system.

Contacting

> write   Send a simple message to the named user, end with
CTRL-D.

The command `mesg n' switches off messages receipt.

> talk Interactive two-way conversation with named user.

Calculation

bc

Calculator.

Syntax

bc [-c] [-l] [file]

Clear

>clear
clear command clears the screen and the puts cursor at
beginning of the first line.

Run Programs In The Background

nohup - run a command immune to hangups, with output to a
non-tty

Synopsis

nohup *COMMAND [ARG]...*

The nohup command runs the command specified by the
Command parameter and any related Arg parameters,
ignoring all hangup (SIGHUP) signals or modifies the process
specified with -p option to ignore all hangup (SIGHUP)
signals.

To run a command in the background even after you log off:

nohup find / -print &

nohup command if added in front of any command will
continue running the command or process even if the system
shuts down or session closes

Transfers files between a local and a remote host.

Use ftp Command

Example a: To connect to the machine test.net, then change
directory , then download the file testfile1:

```
> ftp test.net,

ftp> cd test
  250 CWD command successful.
ftp> get testfile1
ftp> quit
```

to upload the file testfile1

```
ftp> put testfile1
ftp> quit
```

The ftp program by default sends files in ascii (text) format
unless changed to binary mode:

```
ftp> binary
ftp> put testfile1
```

The file testfile1 transferred in binary mode

```
ftp> ascii
ftp> get testfile1
```

The File testfile1 Transferred In Ascii Mode

Loop

```
while TRUE
  do
Command
     sleep 60 seconds
  done
```

Career limiting moves

Do not lists:

I.   Do not Switch off the power on a UNIX system.

II. Don't name your test programs test. It's a UNIX command!

III. Don't use wildcards with rm rm *~ ,rm * ~, deletes all files.

IV. Don't give a file or program or an important file name `core'.

Kill
```
kill - terminate a process
```

SYNOPSIS

```
kill [ -s signal | -p ] [ -a ] [ -- ] pid ...
kill -l [ signal ]
```

Kill Command

Purpose

Sends a signal to running processes.

Syntax

To Send Signal to Processes

kill [-s { SignalName | SignalNumber }] ProcessID ...

kill -SIGNAL PID, where you know the PID of the process.

Programs can choose to ignore certain signals by trapping signals with a special handler.

One signal they cannot ignore is signal 9.

It's a sure way of killing

kill -9 526

Signal 1, or `HUP' can be sent to certain programs by the superuser.

kill -1   <inetd>
kill -HUP <inetd>

which forces `inetd' to reread its configuration file.

kill -20 <PID>   # suspend process <PID>
kill -18 <PID>   # resume process <PID>

What are the access permission of UNIX file/directory? How to Change it?

0 = Nothing
1 = Execute
2 = Write
3 = Execute & Write (2 + 1)
4 = Read
5 = Execute & Read (4 + 1)
6 = Read & Write (4 + 2)
7 = Execute & Read & Write (4 + 2 + 1)

chmod

Changes the permission of a file.

Syntax

chmod [OPTION]... MODE[,MODE]... FILE...

Explain UNIX Set user ID, set group ID, sticky bit?

SUID or setuid: change user ID on execution. If setuid bit is set, when the file will be executed by a user, the process will have the same rights as the owner of the file being executed.

To set the suid permission:

chmod u+s filename

sgid -- this special permission allows the file to be run with the security permissions of the group instead of the permission of the user who ran the program. This can be a source of security problems. The sgid permission is seen as an "S" in the group executable position a long directory listing (ls -l). Has no effect if the file is not executable.

To set the sgid permission:

chmod g+s filename

SGID or setgid: change group ID on execution. Same as above, but inherits rights of the group of the owner of the file. For directories it also may mean that when a new file is created in the directory it will inherit the group of the directory and not of the user who created the file.

Sticky bit. It was used to trigger process to "stick" in memory after it is finished, now this usage is obsolete. Currently its use is system dependant and it is mostly used to suppress deletion of the files that belong to other users in the folder where you have "write" access to.

To set the sticky bit:
chmod o+t dirname

Here is the Numeric representation of the special permissions:

Octal digit	Binary value	Meaning
0	000	setuid, setgid, sticky bits are cleared
1	001	sticky bit is set
2	010	setgid bit is set
3	011	setgid and sticky bits are set
4	100	setuid bit is set
5	101	setuid and sticky bits are set
6	110	setuid and setgid bits are set
7	111	setuid, setgid, sticky bits are set

Textual representation	
SUID	If set, then replaces "x" in the owner permissions to "s", if owner has execute permissions, or to "S" otherwise. Examples: -rws------ both owner execute and SUID are set -r-S------ SUID is set, but owner execute is not set
SGID	If set, then replaces "x" in the group permissions to "s", if group has execute permissions, or to "S" otherwise. Examples: -rwxrws--- both group execute and SGID are set -rwxr-S--- SGID is set, but group execute is not set
Sticky	If set, then replaces "x" in the others permissions to "t", if others have execute permissions, or to "T" otherwise. Examples: -rwxrwxrwt both others execute and sticky bit are set -rwxrwxr-T sticky bit is set, but others execute is not set

UNIX Summary of Commands useful for Forensics

These Commands are referenced from UNIX Manpages.

UNIX

Command	Use
^C	Kill The Job Running In The Foreground
^Z	Suspend The Job Running In The Foregrou
apropos keyword	Match Commands With Keyword In Their Pages
bg	Background The Suspended Job
cat file	Display A File
cat file1 file2 > fileX	Concatenate File1 And File2 To FileX

cd	Change To Home-Directory
cd ..	Change To Parent Directory
cd ~	Change To Home-Directory
cd directory	Change To Named Directory
chmod [options] file	Change Access Rights For Named Fil
command &	Run Command In Background
command < file	Redirect Standard Input From A File
command > file	Redirect Standard Output To A File
command >> file	Append Standard Output To A File
command1 | command2	Pipe The Output Of Command1 To T Command2
cp file1 file2	Copy File1 And Call It File2
fg %1	Foreground Job Number 1
grep 'keyword' file	Search A File For Keywords
head file	Display The First Few Lines Of A File
jobs	List Current Jobs
kill %2	Kill Job Number 2
kill 2152	Kill Process Number 2152
less file	Display A File A Page At A Time
ls	List Files And Directories
ls -a	List All Files And Directories
ls -lag	List Access Rights For All Files
man command	Read The Online Manual Page For A
mkdir	Make A Directory
mv file1 file2	Move Or Rename File1 To File2
ps	List Current Processes
pwd	Display The Path Of The Current Dir
rm file	Remove A File
rmdir directory	Remove A Directory
sort	Sort Data
tail file	Display The Last Few Lines Of A File
wc file	Count Number Of Lines/Words/Cha

	File
whatis command	Brief Description Of A Command
who	List Users Currently Logged In

VI

The VI editor is a screen-based editor used by many UNIX users.
The VI editor has many powerful features to help programmers, developers, testers.
The VI editor uses the full screen, so You may have to set it as per the terminal model you have, for eg if terminal type is vt100:
Set term=vt100
Summary of VI
Starting vi

Command	Description
vi file	start at line 1 of file
vi +n file	start at line n of file
vi +$ file	start at last line of file

Moving Cursor in File	
Left	h
Right	i
Up	k
Down	j
file	
Go to end of file	:$
on chacter forword	:w
One word forword	:W

go to a line number	:line_number
display file info .	^g
Inserting and appending text :	
inserts text to the left of cursor	i
nserts in the beginning of line	I
appends text to right of cursor	a
appends to the end of line	A
Adding new line	
add a new line below the current line	o
adds a new line above the current line.	O
deleting the text :	
deletes text above the text	x

deletes text character on right of cursor	X
deletes line 20	20d
deletes current line	dd
delete till end of current line.	D
Replacing a character & word	
replace the character above the cursor.	r
replces characters until Esc is pressed.	R
replaces the word from cursor to the end indicated by $ sign .	cw
replaces till end of line.	C
Substitute	
subistutes current charcater.	s

substitutes entire line.	S
Undo the last change	
undo last change.	u
undo changes to the current line.	U
Copy and pasting lines	
copys the current line into buffer.	yy
copies 5 lines from the current line.	5yy
pastes the current buffer.	p
Searching	
Searches for the word name in the file	:/name
n continues search forward.	n
N searches backwards	N
Saving	

Saves the text does not quit.	:w
Saves & quit the editor .	:wq!
Save	ZZ
Quit without saving	q!
Search & Replace	s/<search-string>/<replace-string>/g .
Repeating last command	.
Recovering a unsaved vi file.	vi -r filename

Cron

cron is a unix utility that allows tasks to be automatically run in the background at regular intervals by the cron daemon..

Crontab Commands

export EDITOR=vi ;to specify a editor to open crontab file.

crontab -e   Edit your crontab file, or create one if it doesn't already exist.
crontab -l   Display your crontab file.
crontab -r   Remove your crontab file.
crontab -v   Display the last time you edited your crontab file.

Crontab file

A crontab file has five fields for specifying day , date and time followed by the command to be run at that interval.

```
*   *  *  *   * command to be executed

-   -  -  -   -

|   |  |  |   |

|   |  |  |   +----- day of week (0 - 6) (Sunday=0)

|   |  |  +------- month (1 - 12)

|   |  +--------- day of month (1 - 31)

|   +----------- hour (0 - 23)

+------------- min (0 - 59)
```

Crontab Example

```
#minute (0-59),
#|    hour (0-23),
#|    |    day of the month (1-31),
#|    |    |    month of the year (1-12),
#|    |    |    |    day of the week (0-6 with 0=Sunday).
#|    |    |    |    |    commands
0    2    *    *    0,4   /etc/cron.d/logchecker
```

IPC

In UNIX processes communicate with one another using IPC.

This communication is done via shared memory segments, messages queues and semaphores.
Clean all IPC resources when the program is finished.
/usr/bin/ipcs >To display information about active inter-process communication

ipcs –m >To display information about active shared memory segments
ipcs –q > To display information about active message queues
ipcs –s > To display information about active semaphores

ipcs –a > To display information about all active IPC facilities
ipcrm > Remove A Message Queue, Semaphore Set, Or Shared
   Memory Id

Umounting busy devices

To kill process that is keeping filesystem busy

   # fuser -k /mountpoint

   cd - change directory

   ls - list contents of current directory

ls -a - all files
ls -F - show types
ls -l - show long listing, including access permissions

du - disk usage

du - report disk usage in "blocks" (512 bytes)
du - k - report disk usage in kilobytes

exit - Sever connection with the server

chmod - Change permissions (or "mode") of a file or directory

0 no permissions;
1 permission to execute;
2 permission to write;
3 permission to write and execute;
4 permission to read;
5 permission to read and execute;
6 permission to read and write;
7 permission to read, write and execute.

chmod 755 *.html - make all .htmll documents accessible to and executable by the world;

General Rules of Thumb

Directories should be set to **755**, or **777**

Documents should be set to **644**, or **666**

Clear command

clear command clears the screen and puts cursor at beginning of first line.

Nohup command.

Running in the background:

$ nohup ls &

The system responds by telling you about the process identifier, which is usually a multi-digit numeric. You are also informed that the output from the command will be sent to the file **nohup.out**.

Tty command
Tty command will display your terminal.

File Management commands.

Pwd command.
pwd command will print your home directory on screen, pwd means print working directory.

Ls command
ls command is most widely used command and it displays the contents of directory.

head filename by default will display the first 10 lines of a file.

Tail command.
tail filename by default will display the last 10 lines of a file.

More command. more command will display a page at a time
more filename

File command.
File command displays about the contents of a given file

Uniq command.
uniq command removes duplicate adjacent lines from sorted
file while sending one copy of each second file.

sort names | uniq -d will show which lines appear more than
once in names file.

Ftp command (protocol).
ftp command is used to execute ftp protocol using which files
are transferred over two systems.
Syntax is
ftp *options hostname*

Compress command.
Compress command compresses a file and returns the original
file with .z extension

compress options files

Options

- -bn limit the number of bits in coding to n.

- -c write to standard output (do not change files).

- -f compress conditionally, do not prompt before overwriting files.

- -v Print the resulting percentage of reduction for files.

Uncompress command.
Uncompress file uncompresses a file and return it to its original form.

uncompress filename.Z

Save your work:

script filename   Save terminal session to given
filename
                    (Useful to store a.out)

logout/exit/quit/bye   End terminal session

Find

```
find - search for files in a directory hierarchy
```

SYNOPSIS

```
find [-H] [-L] [-P] [path...] [expression]
```

List of expressions:

-atime	last time file was read
-ctime	last time file's owner or permissions were changed
-delete	remove files found
-depth	starts at lowest level in directory tree rather than root given directory
-exec command {} \;	to execute a command; note the required syntax
-group	name or GID
-ls	gives same output as ls -dgils
-mtime	last time file was modified
-name	must be quoted when using wildcards
-newer	find files newer than given file
-ok	use instead of exec to be prompted before command is executed
-perm	specify permissions
-print	displays results of find command
-prune	used when you want to exclude certain subdirectories
-size	rounded up to next 512 byte block or use c to specify k
-type	e.g. f=file d=directory l=link
-user	name or UID

Combining the find and cpio command

```
$ cd /source
$ find . | cpio -pdumv /destination
```

The cpio command is a copy command that will be automatically preserving permissions, times, and ownership of files and subdirectories.

Removing Cores Conditionally

To find and remove core files interactively:

```
find ~ -name core -exec file {} \; -exec rm -i {} \;
```

Copy a tree with cpio and preserve the original owner and group information for the directories and files

```
cd </path/of/source/directory >
find . -depth -print | cpio –pudm </path/of/dest/directory>
```

Find the Hog

If all the space in home directory is used up, here is a way to find the hog:
cd /home
du -ks * | sort -nr | pg

For cleanup:

ls -ls | sort -nr | pg

Searching for old files

If you want to find a file that is 15 days old, use the **-mtime** option:

find . -mtime 15 -print

Reference:
This is an independent and unauthorized notes. No endorsement, sponsorship, affiliation with any other company. Reader is encouraged to buy or take training from related products vedor.References were made from Command Reference manpages, doc portals.

Non Technical/Personal/HR interview: Complimentary

Bottom Line Job interview?

Bottomline: You will learn to answer any questions in such a way that you match your qualifications to the job requirements.

Interview Question?

Example response. Try to customize your answers to fit the requirements of the job you are interviewing for.

What are your greatest strengths?

Articulate.
Achiever.
Organized.
Intelligence.
Honesty.
Team Player.
Perfectionist.
Willingness.
Enthusiasm.
Motivation.
Confident.
Healthy.
Likeability.
Positive Attitude.
Sense of Humor.
Good Communication Skills.
Dedication.
Constructive Criticism.
Honesty.
Very Consistent.
Determination.
Ability to Get Things Done.
Analytical Abilities.
Problem Solving Skills.

Flexibility.
Active in the Professional Societies.
Prioritize.
Gain Knowledge by Reading Journals.
Attention to details.
Vendor management skills.
Excellent Project Management skills.
Self-disciplined.
Self-reliant.
Self-starter.
Leadership.
Team-building.
Multitasking.
Prioritization.
Time management.
Can handle multiple projects and deadlines.
Thrives under pressure.
A great motivator.
An amazing problem solver.
Someone with extraordinary attention to detail.
Confident.
Assertive.
Persistent.
Reliable.
Understand people.
Handle multiple priorities.
Build rapport with strangers.

What are your greatest weaknesses?

I am working on My Management skills.
I feel I could do things on my own in a faster way without delegating
it.
Currently I am learning to delegate work to staff members.
I have a sense of urgency and I tend to push people to get work
done.
I focus on details and think thru the process start to finish and
sometimes miss out the overall picture, so I am improving my skills
by laying a schedule to monitor overall progress.

Had you failed to do any work and regret?

I have No Regrets. I am Moving on.

Where do you see yourself five years from now?

I am looking for a long-term commitment.
I see a great chance to perform and grow with the company.
I will continue to learn and take on additional responsibilities.
If selected I will continue rise to any challenge, pursue all tasks to completion, and accomplish all goals in a timely manner.
I am sure if I will continue to do my work and achieve results more and more opportunities will open up for me.
I will try to take the path of progression, and hope to progress upwards.
In the long run I would like to move on from a technical position to a management position where I am able to smoothly manage, delegate and accomplish goals on time.
I want to Mentor and lead junior-to-mid level reporting analysts.
I want to enhance my management experience in motivating and building strong teams.
I want to build and manage relationships at all levels in the organization.
I want to get higher degree, new certification.

How Will You Achieve Your Goals?

Advancing skills by taking related classes, professional associations, participating in conferences, attending seminars, continuing my education.

Why are you leaving Your Current position?

More money
Opportunity
Responsibility
Growth
Downsizing and upcoming merger, so I made a good, upward career move before my department came under the axe of the new owners.

Why are you looking for a new job?

I have been promoted as far as I can go with my current employer. I'm looking for a new challenge that will give me the opportunity to use my skills to help me grow with the company.

Why should I hire you?

I know this business from ground up.
I have Strong background in this Skill.
Proven, solid experience and track record.
Highest level of commitment.
Continuous education on current technical issues.
Direct experience in leading.
Hands-on experience.
Excellent Project Management skills.
Demonstrated achievements.
Knowledge base.
Communications skills.
Ability to analyze, diagnoses, suggests, and implements process changes.
Strong customer service orientation.
Detail oriented, strong analytical, organizational, and problem solving skill.
Ability to interact with all levels.
Strong interpersonal, relationship management skills.
Ability to work effectively with all levels, cultures, functions.
I am a good team player.
Extensive Technical experience.
Understanding of Business.
Result and customer-oriented.
Strong communication skills.
Good Project and Resource management skills.
Exceptional interpersonal and customer service skills.
Strong analytical, evaluative, problem-solving abilities.
Good management and planning skills.
Good Time Management skills.
Ability to work independently.
I've been very carefully looking for the jobs.

I can bring XX years of experience.
That, along with my flexibility and organizational skills, makes me a perfect match for this position.
I see some challenges ahead of me here, and that's what I thrive on.
I have all the qualifications that you need, and you have an opportunity that I want. It's a 100% Fit.

Aren' t you overqualified for this position?

In My opinion in the current economy and the volatile job market overqualified is a relative term.
My experience and qualifications make me do the job right.
I am interested in a long term relationship with my employer.
As you can see my skills match perfectly.
Please see my longevity with previous employers.
I am the perfect candidate for the position.
What else can I do to convince you that I am the best candidate?
There will be positive benefits due to this.
Since I have strong experience in this ABC skill I will start to contribute quickly. I have all the training and experience needed to do this job. There's just no substitute for hands on experience.

Describe a Typical Work Week?

Meeting every morning to evaluate current issues.
Check emails, voice messages.
Project team meeting.
Prioritize issues.
Design, configure, implement, maintain, and support.
Perform architectural design. Review and analysis of business reports.
Conduct weekly staff meetings.
Support of strategic business initiatives.
Any duties as assigned.Implementation.
Monitor and analyze reports.
Routine maintenance and upgrades.
Technical support.
Deploy and maintain.
Provide day-to-day support as required.
Work with customers and clients.

Documentation.
Standard operating procedures.
Tactical planning.
Determine and recommend.
Plan and coordinate the evaluation.
Effective implementation of technology solutions.
To meet the business objectives.
Participatation in budget matters.
Readings to Keep Abreast Of Current Trends and Developments in the Field.

Are You Willing to Travel?

For the right opportunity I am open to travel.
I'm open to opportunities so if it involves relocation I would consider it.

Describe the pace at which you work?

I work at a consistent and steady pace.
I try to complete work in advance of the deadline.
I am able to manage multiple projects simultaneously.
I am flexible with my work speed and try to conclude my projects on time.
So far I have achieved all my targets
I meet or exceeded my goals.

How Did You Handle Challenges?

Whenever the project got out of track I Managed to get the project schedules back on the track.
Whenever there was an issue I had researched the issues and found the solutions.
We were able to successfully troubleshoot the issues and solve the problems, within a very short period of time.

How do you handle pressure? Stressful situations?

In personal life I manage stress by going to a health club.
I remain calm in crisis.
I can work calmly with many supervisors at the same time.
I use the work stress and pressure in a constructive manner.
I use pressure to stay focused, motivated and productive.
I like working in a challenging environment.
By Prioritizing.
Use time management
Use problem-solving
Use decision-making skills to reduce stress.
Making a "to-do" list.
Site stress-reducing techniques such as stretching and taking a break.
Asked for assistance when overwhelmed.

How Many Hours Do You Work?

I enjoy solving problems and work as much as necessary to get the job done.
The Norm is 40 hour week.

Why are you the best person for the job?

It's a perfect fit as you need someone like me who can produce results that you need, and my background and experience are proof.
As you can see in My resume I've held a lot of similar positions like this one, and hence I am a perfect fit as all those experiences will help me here.
I believe this is a good place to work and it will help me excel.

What are you looking for in a position?

I'm looking for an opportunity where I may be able to apply my skills and significantly contribute to the growth of the company while helping create some advancement and more opportunities for myself.
It seems this organization will appreciate my contributions and reward my efforts appropriately to keep me motivated.

I am looking for job satisfaction and the total compensation package to meet My Worth that will allow me to make enough money to support my lifestyle.

What do you know about our organization?

This is an exciting place to work and it fits my career goals.
This company has an impressive   growth.
I think it would be rewarding to be a part of such a company.

What are your short term goals?

I'd like to find a position that is a good fit and where I can contribute and satisfy my professional desires.

What Salary are you looking for?

Please provide me the information about the job and the responsibilities involved before we can begin to discuss salary.
Please give me an idea of the range you may have budgeted for this position.
It seems my skills meet your highest standards so I would expect a salary at the highest end of your budget.
I believe someone with my experience should get between A and B.
Currently I am interested in talking more about what the position can offer my career.
I am flexible but, I'd like to learn more about the position and your staffing needs.
I am very interested in finding the right opportunity and will be open to any fair offer you may have.

Tell me more about yourself.

I'm an experienced professional with extensive knowledge.
Information tools and techniques.
My Education.
A prominent career change.
Personal and professional values.

Personal data.
Hobbies.
Interests.
Describe each position.
Overall growth.
Career destination.

Why did you leave your previous job?

Relocation.
Ambition for growth.
This new opportunity is a better fit for my skills and/or career ambitions.
To advance my career and get a position that allows me to grow.
I was in an unfortunate situation of having been downsized.
I'm looking for a change of direction.
I want to visit different part of the country I'm looking to relocate.
I am looking to move up the with more scope for progression.

What relevant experience do you have?

I have these XYZ related experience.
I have these skills that can apply to internal management positions et al.

If your previous co-workers were here, what would they say about you?

Hard worker, most reliable, creative problem-solver, Flexible, Helping

Where else have you applied?

I am seriously looking and keeping my options open.

What motivates you to do a good job?

Recognition for a job well done.

Are you good at working in a team?

Yes.

Has anything ever irritated you about people you've worked with?

I've always got on just fine with all my co-workers.

Is there anyone you just could not work with?

No.

Tell me about any issues you've had with a previous boss.

I never had any issues with my boss.

Any questions?

Please explain the benefits and bonus.
How soon could I start, if I were offered the job?

Why did you choose this career?

Life style.
Passion.
Desire.
Interesting.
Challenging.
Pays Well.
Demand.

What did you learn from your last job experience?

I gained experience that's directly related to this job.

Why is there a gap in your resume?

Because of Personal and family reasons I was unable to work for
some time.
Unemployed.
Job hunt.
Layoffs.

How do you keep current and informed about your job and the

industries that you have worked in?

I pride myself on my ability to stay on top of what is happening in the
industry.
I do a lot of reading.
I belong to a couple of professional organizations.
I have a strong network with colleagues.
I take classes and seminars.
I have started and participated in many technical blogs.

Tell me about a time when you had to plan and coordinate a project

from start to finish?

I headed up a project which involved customer service personnel
and technicians.
I organized a meeting and got everyone together.
I drew up a plan, using all best of the ideas.
I organized teams.
We had a deadline to meet, so I did periodic checks with various
teams involved.
After four weeks, we were exceeding expectations.
We were able to begin implementation of the plan.
It was a great team effort, and a big success.
I was commended by management for my managing capacity.

What kinds of people do you have difficulties working with?

I have worked in very diverse teams.
Diversity means differences and similarities with men and women from very diverse backgrounds and culture. It helps us grow as a human being.
The only difficulty was related to work related dishonesty by a person.
He was taking credit for all the work our team accomplished.

What do you want to be in 5 years?

I hope to develop my management skills by managing a small staff.

Ideal career?

I would like to stay in a field of ABC.
I have been good at ABC.
I look forward to ABC.

Responsibilities?

I would expect expanded responsibilities that could make use of my other skills.

Dream job?

Includes all of the responsibilities and duties you are trying to fill.
I also thrive in the fast changing environment where there is business growth.

Skills?

I was very pleased to develop the A, B, C skills that you are seeking

What sets you apart?

Once I am committed to a job or project I take it with tremendous intensity. I want to learn everything I can .I am very competitive and like to excel at everything I do.

If the project not gone as planned?

Backup and identify precautions.

If unable to meet Deadlines?

Negotiate.
Discussion.
Restructure.
Redefine Optimum goal.
Show a price structure.

Interpersonal skill?

I had to learn to say no.
Helpful to other staff.
Help in return.

Improve?

In any job I hold I can usually find inefficiencies in a process, come up with a solution.

What do you feel has been your greatest work-related accomplishment?

Implemented an idea to reduce expenses, raised revenues.

Solved real problems.
Enhanced department's reputation.

Have you ever had to discipline a problem employee? If so, how did you handle it?

Problem-solving skills, listening skills, and coaching skills.

Why do you want this position?

I always wanted the opportunity to work with a company that leads the industry in innovative products.
My qualifications and goals complement the company's mission, vision and values.
I will be able to apply and expand on the knowledge and experience, and will be able to increase my contributions and value to the company through new responsibilities.

Why are you the best person for this job?

I have extensive experience in XYZ (Skill they are looking for)
I'm a fast learner.
I adapt quickly to change.
I will hit the ground running.
I'm dedicated and enthusiastic.
I'm an outstanding performer.
I may be lacking in this specific experience but I'm a fast learner and I'll work harder.

What about Technical writing?

I can convert any complex technical information into simple, easy form.
I can write reports to achieve maximum results.

How versatile you are? Can you do other works?

I am flexible and can adapt to any changing situations.

How do you manage time?

I am very process oriented and I use a systematic approach to achieve more in very less time.
I effectively eliminate much paperwork.

How do you handle Conflicts?

I am very tactful; I avoid arguments and frictions and establish trust and mutual understanding.

What kind of supervisory skills you have?

I make sure that everyone understands their responsibilities. I try to be realistic in setting the expectations and try to balance the work among all.

Any Bad Situation you could not solve?

I've never yet come across any situation that couldn't be resolved by a determined, constructive effort.

Anything else?

I am excited and enthusiastic about this opportunity and looking forward to working with you.

About the Author:

Kumar is an author, educator, and an IT professional with over 18 years of experience in information technology.